T0196441

Shards of Light *and*
Threads of Thought

Shards of Light *and* Threads of Thought

Poems

MARY ELIZABETH LEE

SHARDS OF LIGHT AND THREADS OF THOUGHT
POEMS

iUniverse books may be ordered through booksellers or by contacting:

iUniverse
1663 Liberty Drive
Bloomington, IN 47403
www.iuniverse.com
1-800-Authors (1-800-288-4677)

ISBN: 978-1-4917-9643-6 (sc)
ISBN: 978-1-4917-9644-3 (e)

Library of Congress Control Number: 2016911060

Print information available on the last page.

iUniverse rev. date: 7/29/2016

For my love

Contents

Part 3

Part 1

The timeless in you is aware of life's timelessness
and knows that yesterday is today's memory and tomorrow
is today's dream.
—Kahlil Gibran

Memories

I turned over a mound
of memories and sent
them scurrying through
the foothills of my mind.
Under the cape of an afternoon's
stillness, I watched each spring
for the rows and rows of yellow daffodil
and narcissus often hidden by the drift
of fallen leaves, the first appearances
of separate clusters of black-eyed Susans
nestled along the tree-lined gorges
and the thickets stumbling closer
to the sides of the rushing stream.
I spent my hot summer nights in sticky
stillness, listening to the bullfrog's
call for rain from the shrinking water
hole and the choruses of fiddling crickets
serenading mates in the cooler evening
grasses. Out my bedroom window,
the lonely whip-poor-will called from the
tall pine at the north corner, memories
floating from their cachet like incense
rising as a feather duster of thunder
shook out rumbles in the distance.

Red Rose

Against the tall rye grass,
the red rose
among gray planks
is the lone resident
of the collapsing
wooden structure.
The tenant farmers who
sheltered their families
on the bare plank floors,
sparsely decorated
with straight-back chairs,
have left no lasting mark.
The musty sweat smell
of human beings
has long dissipated
in the gray silence.
Only pieces of an abandoned
calendar blight the bareness
of the graying walls.
Without warning,
a warm breeze ushers
my attention through
the glassless panes
to the Herefords grazing
in the nearby grasses.

Promise of Spring

The dead brown lawn crackles
beneath my feet like the thinly
laid ice of winter in the Deep South.
Each step brings me to the promise
of spring. I tenuously crouch
as my eyes climb the stem
to the swelling tip. No yellow yet,
but soon the daffodils will dot
the landscaped beds as merry
offspring of their sweet mother sun.

Arborescence

From flaxen seed on feathered wing,
a tear from Demeter's eye
springs new white rootlets
downward through ash brown.
Sprigs as wards green
through shimmering dewed ground
in arborescent fullness:
life in a seed.

Happy Lilies

"They must be
touching," he declared
outright when he looked
at the lilies, which
seemed locked in
sorrow. "They
must be touching!"
He replanted all
without another word.
Today when weeding,
I noticed that the lilies
with their long, slim leaves
are touching,
reaching out
in the breezes
for each other,
multiplying
by natural design.

Nature and Sweet Gums

Today I went out to check the bed of
daylilies that had dried up before
their scheduled departure for winter.
I found sweet gum saplings dancing
happily under the dried leaves. They
were everywhere, happily growing
closely together as if family, at least
good friends, in their own miniature
grove. I examined the bed more closely
to find the daylilies also growing once again,
as if the heavy rain after the drought was all
they required. I began to pull up the saplings
that had tried to establish a home in the bed.
The thought that this action by nature
was an effort to ensure survival stopped me.
I reasoned at the same time that their clumping
together and the number of saplings in the bed
would never have made them happy.
They would not be able to thrive in nature's attempt
to make sure her children survived, but
this new sweet gum planting seemed planned,
a desperate effort, to replace the old sweet
gum taken down years earlier. What was
so surprising was the natural planting of so
many young trees! It caused me to think
more sympathetically about the sweet gum
removed from the property. I stopped
with the thought that I had come close
to thwarting nature without knowing
the laws of nature.

Raindrops

Raindrops
on the car window
race nervously
in zigzag formation
up and down
the glass until swept
by the force
of wind
into the fatal line
of extinction
along the rim—
one after the other.

Spring Entourage

Spring's entourage has arrived
with the morning sun, bringing
a noisy troupe of songsters
into the city, twittering, warbling,
and tweeting over quince and crab apple
in song. Greeting each other from every
fence post, double-breasted directors
advise their crews as a symphony
of quavers, tweets, and chirps erupts.
When the warbling stops, the high-wire
acts begin with a host of sparrows sailing
above ground's net from one diagonal
corner post to the other. Business deals
cut in midair on the price of worms,
financial investments, and marriage
counseling sessions. A regular business
meeting held each day with seminars
on encounter groups or public announcements
sponsored by a host of martins, sparrows, and wrens.

Convention

A host of sparrows has
camped out and made their
beds in the neighbor's high-rise
birdhouses. The morning
convention begins early,
often as the sun appears.
Busy executives lecture
their conference-goers
from nearby fence posts
on the price of worms
and the risk of exploration
in the cat's territory
in a symphony
of tremulous sounds,
twittering and tweeting.
Chirping sounds erupt
as they call from street
corners. The trilling stops
for those who entertain.
The trapeze and high-wire
acrobats begin with purple martins
sailing up and around to land
on the electric lines. From one
diagonal corner of the yard to the other,
landing in succession one, two, three, and four,
they are friends for sure.

Velvet Spider

From the photo she showed
me, the face reminded me
of a fruit bat, a monk saki
(an almost extinct monkey),
or maybe a Pekinese, rather pretty.
She went on to explain
that her silky hair to the touch
provides "velvet" to her name.
She continued with the explanation
that in her web the velvet spider
of southern Israel builds
a silk sac for her eggs.
She then squeezes her young
from her egg sac. Before
this hatching is complete,
she has begun her preparation
for disappearing as the mother
by setting her young emerging
from the lair on their own
through the sustenance she prepares
in her abdomen. At this point, I
could not believe my ears.
In their nine days of growing,
the newly hatched consume her
as baby food, leaving only
the husk of her exoskeleton
and her heart, perhaps,
as I have to believe,
as the purist expression
of natural love.

Winter in the Deep South

When the sweet gums cling
to but a few withered balls, and
all but the tall green pines
and the red-berried hollies
have gone underground, leaving
only bare structures like so much
structured steel in artistic form,
the cold invades quietly by night
while the farmhouse sleeps. It glides
around corners, through crevices and
cracks, displacing the warmth as it spreads.
Like an adventurous ghost, it floats
under, over, and around the bed and bedcovers,
skimming over the other furnishings, finally
hiding behind the window shades to await
the morning risers. Hostage-taking cold
is merciless in a farmhouse well ventilated and
sparsely heated by one wood burner. There are
no six ways about it. A nose can get red cold,
and hands and feet can freeze to break. Five
heavy quilts, long stored generation after
generation and piled on one bed, threaten to smother
or crush, yet they fail to keep the body heat in and
the winter's cold out. Morning wakes too early,
and only kitchen sounds and gnawing hunger
urge the feet to scout for warmth on the cold floor.

Winter Art

The Deep South is having
its first cool weather
in November. The photo
with its striking frozen beauty
from Mount Adams in northern
New Hampshire in the local newspaper
caught my eye. I am not sure what
the motivation of the newspaper was
for printing the photo, but what ensued
was a lesson for me about the artistic
partnership between wind and water
in the colder regions and the canvas
winter provides. The supercooled water
droplets blown into the solid sign in the photo
formed the appearance of the long flowing hair
of a woman. Her windblown locks
streamed behind her, art on the windward
side called rime ice in an ice kingdom
that challenged my concept of beauty.

The Place for Window Glass

Midmorning the two
meet daily with respectful
interest. The sun has warmed
the brick window ledge
to the young brown lizard's
liking. The raised window
blind gives the cat a nice
view. The two stare at
each other, knowing
the adventure possible.
The visit goes on for
a few minutes as the
lizard, now green, makes
its way to the other end
of the ledge. The sight
of this beautiful being
sets the cat to trembling
with the passion for the hunt.
Only a thin pane of window
glass these sunny mornings
makes them friends, until
tomorrow when they will meet again.

Lesson in Safety

We braked the car quickly
for the sight before us.
There on the left side
of the roadway was a group
of fluffy young goslings
lined up about to cross
the street, led by a large,
big-breasted gander. As if cued
that it was safe to cross, the large
leader put out one foot to touch
the pavement, as if checking
the temperature, and then
stepped lively across the street
with the young ones following
in a straight line like schoolchildren
taught to hold on to the shirt of the one
before them. One young gosling
missed the cue to cross with the others,
as he was busy working in the grasses nearby.
The goose of the gander, while bringing up
the rear, hesitated for a moment until the straggler
realized he was being left behind. He quickly
joined the march to the other side of the street
as the mother goose herded the young ones to safety.

Rats

I put out some stale bread
for the birds in the back
of the house, only to see
a small rat eating the bread
and swinging on a tiny limb
of the weeping yaupon in
Ratatouille style as if in his own
kitchen. I knew then that I had
a problem with gluttonous rats
akin to the ones in the movies. This
young one had broken the unspoken
truce and was having too much fun
out in the open, as if he were the lead
actor of a group of rogue rodents.
We are under a rain forecast for a week,
giving them a short reprieve, but
as soon as the rain stops, I will put
the mothballs out about three feet
a part all around the house, disrupting
the community of another creature
in the city, this time a group of rogue
rat actors on stage.

Scavengers

A short distance ahead, a dozen, give
or take one or two more, large beautiful
blackbirds were busy cleaning up
the roadkill of an opossum. As the car
approached, the two larger leaders
grabbed the carcass with their beaks
and then dragged the remains
off the street to the grass nearby
with the young, smaller ones running off
the road behind them. What a beautiful,
intelligent action that cleared the road for the cars
traveling the boulevard and provided a healthful
lunch for the birds obeying their calling! Most
would say the most revolting bird of creation
is the scavenger. But that description fails
to depict what I saw this late sunny morning
on the way to my lunch.

Deserted Farmland

From the roadside
as far as I can see,
encroaching green thickets
crowd the sunbaked
and weed-filled farmland.
A rusting hoe left on a sagging
fence is the one clue of owners now gone.
Isolated clusters of summer's bitterweed
form their own colony of yellow and
surround the farmhouse. The tall pines sway
to the rhythm of the wind, as up above
the clouds joust in overstuffed free-form.
Watching the sun float behind the thickets
and squeeze between the green trees and the blue sky,
I feel a breeze nudge me and I turn back to the car.

Bully

The two met for lunch at noon
under the oak by the canal.
The mockingbird hopped cheerfully
along the sidewalk as if playing hopscotch, stopping
in a deliberate stance to pick up crumbs in the shade.
Without provocation, he rushed like a taxiing plane
on the runway at the other mockingbird, who, undaunted,
continued to stare with intent into the grasses
bordering the sidewalk. Thwarted, the truculent one
swept up to the overhanging *Ligustrum*, cursing loudly,
and then darted down again at the second mockingbird.
In repeated charges, he ran at the second one
twice more and then once at a sparrow,
who continued lunch undisturbed,
causing me to wonder at the birds' tolerance
of this bully.

A Breeze

It was a beautiful sunny day in May,
with animal-creating clouds that
could be anything the imagination
wished. As far as one could see
up the street, a strange, seemingly
living thing was moving across
the road. It was light tan
with orange markings, perhaps
two kittens in a tousle. As the car
neared the spot, I discovered, much to my delight,
that it was clearly a breeze hitching a ride
in a plastic bag, doing somersaults
across the street and into the ditch,
head over heels.

Fly

The fly visiting me
at the unlikely site
of a restaurant did
not sit down for dinner
on my food or fly
close to my face. He chose
my right shoulder
to rest and to explore
with front feelers in midair.
From the first sighting,
I thought of the stops
in his short life, which
for him could have seemed
very long. If a senior fly,
he could have been needing
a resting place or hospice
care at the end of his life.
This special spirit continued
to favor my right shoulder.
I wondered if he were the messenger
of someone trying to reach me
from the other side. Shooed from
my right shoulder, he simply went
to the left shoulder, soon returning
to the right. At this point, I left him
where he chose to be—
my right shoulder,
within hearing distance
of my ear, just in case.

The Song of the River

Inspired by a piece of art placed alongside the waterfront of Baton Rouge to capture the songs of the Mississippi River

Your soprano voice
rises from the headwaters
in Minnesota, reaching
a crescendo along
the winding journey
to the Gulf of Mexico,
telling us in waves of song
that you are one
of the world's major
river systems. Your
voice deepens as you
remind us that you
are the fourth largest
watershed from the Allegheny
Mountains to the east and
the Rocky Mountains
to the west. I can hear you
surging in a baritone shuffle,
lapping the banks and
sides of boats as you roar
toward the Gulf, your length
the fourth longest in the world.
You need no conductor as you sway
in harmony with the voices
of the cities that rely on you
for their water supply.
In waves of tenor rolls,
you voice your support

of the largest port district
in the world located
along the Mississippi
Delta. I hear the joy
in your serenade
of the species of fish,
and for the migratory birds
that use the river basin
as their flyway. Everywhere,
with your singing, floodplains
host hundreds of amphibians, mussels,
and reptiles. Let us join you
in song. Sing, great river, Sing!
Sing of your world
as you roll toward the Gulf
on the way to your destiny
as the great contributor
to wetland development.

More

When
the trees
grow restless
in the late afternoon
and sway their limbs
to the silent music
of the wind,
I know
there is
more to know,
more to see,
more to live for.

Snapshots of Nature

a splash of red
against a backdrop of green
a rose

cannas blooming
in a bed of pine straw
in a world of suns

flaxen seeds
a tear from Demeter's eye
new rootlets sprouting

sprigs sprout
through ground in shimmering dew
life in a seed

the cascading branches
of berries on the weeping yaupons
make a refuge for the birds

the weeping yaupons
draped in red berries remain
nature's holiday tree

Part 2

Life's experiences provide roots for education
while education becomes merely so much foliage.
—Elizabeth Lee

Artisan

for Judy

From the early age of eight,
she has searched like an avid prospector
for the gems she knows by name,
stored in the drawers and walls
of her muse. Guided by her
own moonbeams of design,
she travels new distances,
new depths created from
the lives of rocks. Anything
from nature's gallery,
including creations in wood; soaps
or candles from other artisans;
and her own creations from
precious/semiprecious
stones, speak a language
the customers in her shop
understand. The talk of
customers affirms her craft
and its goodness, enabling
her to climb another
ladder of natural stone
for the dig in nature's
cauldron of gems.

Craftsman

This able workman has been on the job
for one and a half weeks. With the
Hephaestus touch, he has cleverly
designed solutions to the problems that
have come up, making himself the grand
craftsman of the tile kingdom. The sound
of the saw cutting the tile is mitigated by the sound
of his radio and his singing. He breaks
into a sing-along with the radio when he
has come to a stopping point or is close
to finishing a part of the project, such as
the glass tile or the shower floor. Surely
a lesser musician than Apollo, he is still
fitting for the inspiration. When he has
reached his expectations, he whistles
the songs that rival the Sirens' songs,
drawing his skills from those craftsmen
who have traveled this world before. I have
always held a fondness for a craftsman
who knows his craft, inspired by the past.

Modern Paul Bunyan

He hails as a hero to many and scales
the jobs of others without pause.
His restlessness, like that of a hungry
mountain lion, pushes him to help
others and to keep himself busy.
He mows lawns or applies a coat
of paint to houses suffering from
contention with paint-chip sorrow.
Ask this former military policeman
a question and, with a few clicks
on his laptop, he will have the answer.
His acumen spreads like soft butter
between getting the best price
on a home to fathering two in need.
He will scout for lunch or light his grill
to cook up tasty meals for guests. He
never seems to tire, and spins a tale
worthy of Paul Bunyan folklore. Only when
he comes inside and slips down on the floor
to watch TV beside his two dogs and cat,
all loved more than the blue ox named Babe,
will you see his eyes close for a short nap.

Earth Girl

Dressed in orange shirt, brown capri
pants, and a wide-brimmed hat,
she ventures out early to take care of her
imaginary duties. She flutters
from lawn to lawn in the neighborhood
with a purpose as real as that of a butterfly
but which remains unclear to observers.
Her imaginary tasks may take her two
or three blocks from her home. When she
determines the spot to receive her special
treatment, her small frame lights
like a monarch butterfly, her clothes
ballooning out in shades of black, brown,
and orange on a sea of green in the yards
of neighbors and friends. She drills down
with her fingers to search for the secrets
of the grass in the lawn, humming and singing
to comfort Earth. She, so intent
on her task, only occasionally
notices passing motorists, and when she does,
she smiles innocently and waves.

Stars

A decade ago,
I caught the stars
in the eyes of a woman
I had always loved.
Her thick black hair
framed her blue-green eyes,
many years young,
making them sparkle with life.
I remember the times at dusk
when she'd say, "Listen
to the whip-poor-will."
We'd ask, "What is it saying?"
And she would tell us,
"Chip flew outta the white oak."
I remember those cold mornings
when she ousted us out of bed
with, "Get up! Quick! Jack Frost is here!"
My first memory of the awakening
was annoyance, not because she had
awakened me, but because I had expected
Jack Frost to be an interesting person.
Instead, as my eyes followed
the direction of her finger to the outside,
I saw Jack Frost's icy white all over the ground
and I shivered. Only later did
I understand she was teaching us
about the beauty of nature.

Butane Heater

The button on top
of the gas heater
continues to snap
with each press
of the finger.
The whishing
and the acrid smell
of the burning gas
is the goal, but the heater has
lost its way or fails to have
the strength to reach
a slurp of gas to create
the blue flame. The owner
with patience continues
to press the switch
to cause the union
of air and gas. With luck
and fortitude, it may finally
catch like its owner and
burn another warm thought.

Someone Else

She comes out of the jungle
of tangled vines, an explorer still
lost in the sum of her years. She is
a new person whom her children
must learn anew. A fresh breeze
from a thought can prompt her
and cause her to return almost
to herself to the delight of her loved ones.
At this point, she wants to hear agreement
from her children with her understanding
of her newly discovered world. She is now
a twenty-year-old woman, wondering where
her husband is, but if she still knows her children
by name, all is forgiven and there is hope that they,
once again, will reach the person they love.

Attendant

Her young hand closed gently
around the soft frail hand,
once so firm. The thin, blue-tinted skin
was much warmer than she had thought,
but still very frail. She remembered,
as she saw in those warm eyes
the innocence of hopeful youth.
She swam in the wisdom of those eyes
as she had swum in the womb.
She turned to say,
"Love is ageless."

Hot Buffalo Wings

Around seven in the evening,
a sandy-haired stranger and
a local known by those
at the Anchor Bar joined
the small drinking group.
The banter ensuing between
the two latecomers spilled
over into the space as they
saddled up to the bar with
the other patrons. When
the attendant took a tray
of red buffalo wings from
the refrigerator, the stranger
ordered a plate. She asked if
he were sure, because the red
pepper sauce used on the wings
was very hot. He told her that
where he came from he
was used to hot food.
He bragged, "I drink
Louisiana Tabasco sauce straight
from the bottle." She gave
him what he ordered. He ate
one wing and then the second one,
and suddenly a change came over
his face that everyone in the bar
recognized. He turned beet red,
sweating profusely and trying
to speak in squeaks that sounded
like baby mice. His friend just looked
at him as if to say, "She said they were hot."

The stranger pushed the plate
to his friend, who pushed it
to the next patron, who pushed
the plate to the next, looking
for another risk taker.

The Card

card (colloquial): a person who attracts attention by
his wit, eccentricity, etc.

He comes from an unknown house of cards.
He is a card by birth—sometimes an ace,
sometimes a king. He can be a suit of cards
or a wild hand. He soars as the king of hearts,
the jack of spades, or the queen of diamonds. He's
never quite sure which suit he will assume
for the play. Watch out when he dresses
for other festivals, confusing the confinement
of the suit. He may still be the queen
of hearts or the king of diamonds.
In trick-making games of rugby,
he may offer a no-trump suit to
his minions at charge and camouflage
the plays through passes of decks and
hands. When out of suits of hearts,
diamonds, or clubs, he is more devious,
surprising those still in the game
as the joker of the deck.

In a Calendar Year

Her beauty belied her strength,
a strength strong like a stone wall
when she had a mind to do something
or felt she had to draw from it. She could
bake sweet milk biscuits for breakfast,
milk the cows, Jersey and Blanche,
and be in the fields by daybreak.
With sweat streaming from the blue-black hair,
she tended the children, peeled the potatoes,
snapped the beans, did the wash, and hung the clothes
to dry on the fence, if the clotheslines were full.
She found the energy to start dinner and rush
to stretch barbed wire to keep the cows out of the feeding pastures.
In the spring, she helped load calves for the sale barn.
Working twelve hours a day in July, she picked
and canned string beans, corn, beets, tomatoes—
seven days a week until there were no more
vegetables or containers. In October, she loaded
and unloaded baled hay for the winter feed. In
the cold months she broke the ice on the pond
so the cows could drink, pitched hay for the cows,
and checked the hay and feed supply. If she were
the gauge of endurance, could any man measure up?

Politician

He lives in gripping fear
between the present and the future.
His faith twists in falsely held
tales of the past. His confidence
is shaky these days because
he does not see God speaking
from the burning bush,
blinding the wicked of sight,
turning disobedient ones
into pillars of salt,
or causing fire to rain down
on cities. To the hills
of sentiment he rushes
to grab selectively
time-blurred relics. He polishes
them like gems with new
rhetoric to bring them into the present
as new. Only then can he
protect himself and his
supporters from the mental
monsters when the moon is full
and the werewolf howls.

Touring Adventure

She rolls out touring weekly
in her motorized wheelchair
along the neighborhood
streets. Tufts of white hair fall
like peaks of whipped cream
above the back frame of the chair,
her dark clothes draped
like melted chocolate covering her
in warmth. She waves joyfully
to the drivers of passing cars.
With her on sunny days is her
Jack Russell terrier without a leash,
his trot bound by his responsibility.
This midmorning he runs
in front of her, squarely
in the middle of the width
of the wheelchair, her horse
leading the surrey. The invisible
leash of affection keeps them
connected, and between them
the speed of the chair
at the right distance maintains
the appearance of a well-planned adventure.

Angelic Spirit

for Jessica

When happy thoughts brighten her world,
she floats into focus, her long white hair
cloaking her shoulders and forming the wings
of her future flight. She is the unsung angel
because of the shyness that consumes her.
She enters the world to watch and to observe
with a smile and then to make a quick return to her refuge.
With her is her fearless feline, following her
in its blindness along the outside walls of the room.
When the days grow longer, she finds a couple
of hours here and there, when time is hers,
to slip through her window to smoke her
thoughts for the day. She and her feline friend
stand as a pair that can take diversity
and share any dare.

Dark Brown Recliner

Its brownishness wraps its arms
around him as if a monster from one
of his favorite science fiction movies. It consumes
him as he disappears, leaving behind only
the protest sounds of sleep, sinking deeper and deeper
into the world of peaceful leather. It entices him
and keeps him captive despite his protests
that he should exercise more as he sinks deeper
and deeper into the darkness of dreamy sleep.
Its hold on him allows him to stir, only to find
a more restful spot, or to eye the clock for the time
before he slips away to a secret dreamland.
When the chair grows tired of him, it burps him
upright. He returns from the odyssey a little
groggy, but a nicer man than the one who left.

Rose

You are much like
a fragrant splash of red
against a backdrop of green,
a rose
whose sweetness
is moderated
only
by the thorns
of its growth.

Part 3

We never escape the schoolyard;
the kids grow only taller.
—Elizabeth Lee

.

Protocol

*Navajo woman Mae Chea Castillo appeared at the
White House and delivered a speech to President
Ronald Reagan on April 27, 1983*

It is not good
for an eighty-year-old
Navajo woman
from New Mexico
to tell the king
the song he does
not want to sing—
or what he does
not know about
the hard times in the 1980s
and suffering people
everywhere.
Protocol is the thing
to remember
in the visit,
not the need
to educate
the busy king.
Take back
your sincerity
and your gifts
of blanket, basket,
and wise song
you sing and save
them for a warmer day.

Her Baby, the Woman

Every mother's daughter came
home today wearing cherry-red lips,
three rhinestone studs in her right ear,
three shades of blue eye shadow,
and three tattoos of woe.
The mother, finding herself
somewhere between eighteen and
sixty-five, was reminded of what she feared.
Her baby, the woman, is thirteen going
on eighteen, and a woman's declaration
of independence is near.

Cold Babble

Cold babble
about young death
during warm years,
about death self-imposed,
indiscriminately assigned,
turned indignant.
"Did you go?" you would ask.
I went, but not for the few Longfellow lines
about *tugged heartstrings* or for
the weak message—as weak
as plain coffee to mocha,
as water to red wine,
as tea to bourbon,
and as ineffective as
the priestly attempt
to release the guilt.
I wondered if Blake's God meant it so.
"What did you think?" you would ask
if you were here, as flippant about death
as you pretended to be about life,
full of quips, verbal jabs, happy smiles.
You always walked like a battery-run clown doll,
throwing your weight from side to side
as you threw your savvy, your quick wit,
your comic gumption, your common sense
in its uncommon way. But circumstance
was your fate, and your dejected spirit moved
uncommonly away in the wail
of the whistle of the train
that chilly afternoon in early February
on Mardi Gras.

Slanted Glance

I invite you in
with a slanted glance
that lasts too long
to be casual. Once
you are in,
you make yourself
at home. You leave
me behind, before tea,
forgetting I invited you.

Forgetting Old Loves

Be careful of pitching your tent
in midair. How hard it might be
to secure it to ground stakes—
the flapping, the whipping,
the stretching of the canvas
by angry winds could split seams,
ruining all—and you might
from such a lofty berth fall.
Do not take lightly the bishop's impeachment
of Yeats' Crazy Jane: "Love has pitched"
your tent in "The place of excrement; / For
nothing can be sole or whole / That has not
been rent." The foulness you will know,
and you will then have the gall from your
old tent to go, an escapee at night. From the
nightmare you will find yourself where you might—
whole again, light of heart, light of spirit.

Haunted House

I remember.
I think I do.
Bare weathered walls.
A rent house.
The Old Cranford house,
they called it,
where I ate
from a jar of snuff.
Later, as a teenager,
when I passed the aging house
I'd sometimes stop.
From the sagging wire fence
I'd steal a look.
Its hollow eyes
still spook me.

Filament of Life

On hot summer days like today,
the clouds leave too many
smudged shadows on the grass.
But, then, I have not always been
aware of smudges darkening vision.
It's hard to see the wispy silk
filament of life when the sun
is shadowed by thunderclouds.
Faint red, blue, and green casts
of prism light are too soft to catch,
and I fail to see the beauty. Only when
I feel the yarn brush against
my leg, tapping faintly like the soft
paw of a cat, do I finger it, milking
the tangles and storing it to begin
the spin again of the yarn to make
more thread to sew the gown of
life. There is much to learn about
soft silk threads and smooth cotton webs,
to understand about soft skill and smooth
technique, to touch with a mother's wisdom,
a sister's imagination, in the simple winding
of the thread of life in the spinning
of the yarn, thin as air.

Upon Reading Dugan's "Mock Translation"

My thoughts are less robust,
less inquiring, and foggier
than the day that dawns. On this walk,
the fog hangs low and I feel
the mist on my face. I cannot see
through the thicket in my head
blinding my thoughts. I have watched
the people I know, the students I teach,   .
searching for the light that relights the candle
in the dark to make the way clearer. I walk
with the trees and marvel at their network
of activity from their massive limbs, but their
voices are muted. Erato and Apollo have mislaid
their torches and have abandoned us along
this lonely road of unclaimed spirits. I tuck
the frustration under my rib cage to await
a new day. Let Walt Whitman and Emily
Dickinson be the purveyors of literary tradition.
An impossible grouping as it may seem,
all is but a foreshadowing wind of few answers.

Unruly Hours

Tiresome, unruly hours,
their fretful, hungry minutes
in tow, fray sensitive nerve endings
with each second's whimper.
Whispering wings of thought
touch heavy eyelids and brush
the face, slipping into the shadows
of a warm cup of milk like a mosquito
hawk skimming across still water.
Soft musical whispers from the dishwasher
and the clothes dryer drown out the weariness
for a chamomile moment, while
the hours hang from the ceiling,
taunting with each cycle.

Cloaked Voice

Late one summer afternoon in an old city far away,
a tired man sat down to rest on the dusty steps
of the large limestone building. A light sleep
came over him, and he dreamed of a soft, soothing
voice, failing to see that the comforting sound
belonged to a feminine form that looked his identical.
He walked with the white-draped figure into the building.
"Oh yes, look at these great ones," he said
as the two moved slowly from display to display.

What men had thought
What men had seen
What men had said
What men had done
in the antiqued years

There, in perfect form, were
Men, the pontiffs, so divine;
Men, the conquerors, so fierce;
Men, the thieves, so bold;
Men, the alchemists, so daring;
Men, the philosophers, so inspired;
Men, the governors, so lawful.

The cloaked voice replied, "Shouldn't there be more?
Half sometimes is all one can see.
Sighting of the whole is lost and not to be,
except as haunts—only haunts—in the minds
of those who know what should be."

The man awoke from his dream, wondering at its significance.

Upon Reading Langston Hughes' "As I Grew Older"

I realize now
the source
of my sadness.
It is personified.
I know it
for the first time.
I know it by name.
It is not the same wall
in similar sense
as that which Hughes experienced,
but it is still a wall that teaches me
my place in society. Until now,
I had been unable to objectify
my sadness.
I carry it within me
just below my navel,
sometimes on my left shoulder
or squarely on my back.
It causes a limiting
sadness, appearing
often, but always when
I drop my guard.
The wall has risen
and fallen in my life,
only to rise again
brick by brick,
structuring my mind
with the words of Pink Floyd:
"just another
brick in the wall."
It is the sadness,

the rejection, I felt
when I was excluded,
overlooked, and unseen
amid the conversation
of the men around the fire
while the woman prepared the food.
I was excluded from my father's domain.
I too grew older,
became too old,
too young,
too female,
too male—
not right enough
to go with my dad
to the neighbors'
for men's talk,
too something
at twelve to climb
the sweet gum,
too something,
a tomboy,
too something
but deserving
of the dumb row
for girls
in the seventh grade,
too something
or not enough
to keep
my own credit cards
and my surname
when I married,
and not enough
to be paid
what the college history teacher
across the hall received

because he had a family,
not enough
for my salary
to be included
in the mortgage application,
and finally,
too vulnerable
to go alone
at night
to the shopping mall
or to a movie.
You see,
I am female,
and society
will not let
me forget it—
and this wall has
split my world
and chipped
my words
with anger.

Soft Words

Deep
from within
the cavern
comes
the scream
echoing off
the walls
of my mind,
condensing
in drops
of fear,
covering
my body
cold.

His unexpected kiss on my hand,
the cup of hot tea on a cool day,
the glass of iced tea on a warm day,
whichever may work best on
what is bothering me, is not
always enough to calm my panic.
I have to ask, "What tribe do
you come from?" I crawl on his
chest and hold his face in my hands to ask,
"Who are you?" because—
because I read too many
statistics and stories
about the worldwide
Saturday night sport
of raping, beating, killing
females to know—
This horror leaves me
cold and empty,

and I need
his soft words
on my body
and his soothing
strokes on my spirit
to assure me
he isn't
the enemy.

Change in Big Easy

The sky thickened and darkened. For hours
the rain fell in endless sheets. The howling wind
remained, a screeching monster pushing debris
through windows and doors as the raging water
swallowed landfall. The long gusts of wind
finally halted, but the worst was yet to come.
The churning mass of water pushed powerful
surges through channels, breaking through levees,
splintering homes and businesses into tons of rubbish,
leaving rescued citizens dispelled and looking for safety
anywhere else but there. The music of the musicians
drained with the water from the streets of the city.
Joy and revelry followed, leaving emptiness
on the street corners and in the clubs. The old ways
of the city and the citizens who lived them disappeared
in mountains of useless debris, hauled away and forgotten.
In their place, ideas like wild weeds, once heresy,
for remaking the city rerooted, and sprouted
in new city districts with new people.

Downturn

There's been a turndown for me
this economical morning. So it seems
from what I read between the blurred lines.
Between you and me, a turndown is more
than a rolling fold of bedcoverings
across the chest, binding breath, smothering sleep.
A sudden downturn, the news calls it:
a malaise, a fear taken from the office
in blocks of frozen platitudes I hear
melting in the surrounding walls.
This turndown results from a downturn
coming out of nowhere, blowing fiercely
like a northeaster, chilling, whipping
cold rain against the window panes,
gusting, upsetting lawn chairs,
the table umbrella, unleashing garbage cans.
Through the window panes I look
for the reason, the need to understand changing
fortunes, the closing and moving of dreams.
The topography of sand and sun
in the windows of empty houses remains.
Listening daylong to the media translations:
exports are down, imports flooding,
unions pressuring, minds atrophying.

At Fifty

On a sunny spring day I hand-washed
and hung my thoughts out to dry
in the strong breezes of contentment.
The gusts from the wings of eager thoughts
fanned the edges into smooth textures
and grouped them in soft surging swirls
like fireflies in the dullness of evening light.
The bluing in the breezes whitened
the yellow stains of living on my thoughts
and gave them strength, making them
kinder and crisper. When I removed
the clothespins and brought them in
to fold into lavender boxes to keep
the sweet fragrance strong,
my thoughts stood tall like a bed
of purple irises.

Courage

Out over the water
where the seam joins the sky,
I wonder what courage
Columbus had to sail over
the edge and back, yet
respect I must those who
fear being more than the physical
that restrains them. There is
something haunting in the dancing
to forgotten rhythms, haunting
in the edge that lies out there
in the savanna tall grasses
at the blade's edge, the shifting
cutting edge of fear in you and me.
It inhibits, numbs the mind
like pinpricking nerve pain,
the unseen of the seen, the waking
from the sleeping, from birth to death.
To see beyond the earth's rim
where the stars launch and disappear
is to wait a lifetime for the awakening
of that which surfaces so close
but refuses to speak at the edge
of the reptilian brain.

My Own Worst Enemy

True to my nature, I will lease
an automobile rather than
wait until I can afford to pay
in cash. The lease allows me
to drive a more expensive car
than I can normally afford because
it costs less to lease per month than
it costs to buy. I buy denim pants,
up to six in one color, rather
than wait until I wear out a pair
of white or black. I retired a few
months early rather than wait until
I had reached the maximum age.
I reasoned that I might not live
long enough to recoup any advantage
I might accrue by waiting until later.
And so I am tempted
by happy hour, to the detriment
of exercise. When trying to lose weight,
I cannot resist having a cup of gelato
instead of keeping to my diet. I find myself
surfing the Internet instead of completing
the poem on my desk. Just as puzzling,
I did not feel guilty and was not even
aware of what I was doing until reading
the article about this subject in a science
magazine. I am my own worst enemy.
And now research proves that we are all
tempted to take an immediate reward
over a future reward. Today I feel
a small stone in my shoe reminding me
of the guilt every time I think about
skipping exercise.

At the Foot of the Trees

I sat in my youth in the days
of my dreams where everything
was more than it seemed. I felt
a kinship with the pine thickets
and the blackberry bushes growing
on the outskirts. I marveled at the beautifully
white spotted trunks of sycamores that provided
shade and the draping arms of oaks that screened
the schoolhouse from the street, realizing that
from trees we garner much value that extends
beyond amazement. Then as now, I walk
along nature trails crowded by curious pines
to smell the sweetness of dried pine needles
with the thought to rake up a few bales
to place around the plants in my flower beds
and to collect some pinecones to paint
silver, gold, and red for the holidays.

Choices

Cover or to cover not
        hair
        body
        feet

Paint or to paint not
        cheeks
        lips
        nails

Have or to have not
        in schools
        in homes
        in meetings

Is or is not
        homosexual
        heterosexual
        transgender or bisexual

Believe or to believe not
        Bible/Talmud
        Koran
        Tipitaka/The Veta

Choose or choose not
        love
        forgiveness
        peace

Zero

I am zero,
the nonentity
between the force
of all negative
numbers and all
positive numbers.
Between the two
at the point of departure
is reckoning, to stand
there as martyr or symbol,
the invisible control
of conflict between the two
while the zephyr cools
the fires of conflict
at ground zero.

Obsession

In my mind's clandestine chambers
of desire, the nightmare nights of cliffs
and sinking sands, I have grown strong
that which will not release me. It enthralls me,
sets my head spinning, engendering me with
promise to do until time is not, to act until
the act is not, to change the bird-dog routine,
the mind game of sport and fun. I grasp
at the threads of thought enlaced in the clouds
of confusion. Woven windows wide deny
light to the coil that springs from the curse
of the raging fire, and I dare to be there
to await the ashes.

Companion

She moves like a racer
on a ten-speed bike
in her sleek black body built
like a promising racehorse
with her hindquarters
sitting high. Her large
green eyes squint to show her
deepest affection, yet she rejects
all romantic advances from the locals.
After early breakfast, she schedules
her day around sunbathing and
punctuates her late morning with naps
on the carport before she baby-sits the terrier
and spanks him for streaking out the gate
past her to freedom. She notes all visitors
in the neighborhood, checking unfamiliar
cars and trucks, watching the men take down
the oak or guarding for days at a time
the grapevines in the backyard
from mockingbird raids. In early mornings and
in late afternoons, she accompanies me
to inspect the plants, talking the whole time
about her likes and dislikes. Her time is hers,
and your time will be hers too should she need it.

Space for Lease

The strip mall sits empty and bare,
blank windows staring out on the
parking lot waiting, void of any
activity. No more orders are picked up
from the space once called a Lebanese
restaurant. No signs remain of nails
painted and polished next door
after fifteen years in business
with many happy customers. No products
to soothe and to beautify skin appear three
doors down in the darkened window.
Only empty spots remain where
the citrus trees had displayed greenery
and comfort to those stopping to eat
and shop. Fruit trees without the caring master
to feed and water them could not retain
their dress in green or bear fruit for the owner
of the real estate.

The Game of Conversation

The six women meet almost every
month at a local restaurant to keep
the personal fires burning. All but
one is retired from the local college.
As the members arrive one at a time,
the excitement swells and rises like
balloons let loose in an open sky,
and then the real conversation begins.
With the last one seated, the chirping
of stories and the twilling of jokes begin
the game of conversation. Everyone
waits for a turn to tell her story
for the month. Some have worked together
at the college in the same unit,
guaranteeing much to share
and questions to be asked. The others
listen and, when they recognize parts
of the story, jump in trilling their
bits, dipping comments like chips
in sauce to pepper the pleasure.
It is clear from their sharing of good books
and the latest news that the affection
is strong among them as they weave
their lives together in a strong fabric
of love and trust.

Gift of Soap

The handmade bar has worn
so thin that it is almost
transparent. The remaining
three perfectly formed red roses
continue to provide days of
mulberry fragrance during
my morning bath, a nursery
rhyme memory of dancing
around in circles singing,
"Here we go 'round the
mulberry bush, the mulberry
bush, the mulberry bush."
It takes me back to the fragrances
that soothed my memories
of red roses in bloom, and starry
white fragrant clematis
in a garden of fragrance.
I will miss this pleasurable
gift of mulberry soap.

The Flute

The sounds of the flute rise
like the bouquet of vintage
burgundy. The melody circles
rising and falling like the fragrance
of faint honeysuckle. Like a bee taking
nectar deep within, sleeping spirits awake
and curl upward from the piercing.
Ancient fires burning within release
the flames where the red and yellow
colors dance along the fringes
of the universe, burning
away the fear of the night.

No New Myths

Our early ancestors on those dark nights
watched the eclipse, looking for signs
to make their truths. They studied
the full moon for the right time to till
the land and to plant their seeds.
They read the stars to write the stories
of their gods and goddesses
to explain what they could not
understand. They sought to comprehend
the mystery of the ever-changing sky
and to provide order to the chaos of living.
They too must have certainly seen
the alignment of the planets and
meteors shooting across the sky. They were
so amazed that they created the myths we know well.
Today's astronomers have identified the planets
by name and are fascinated with the alignment
but do not feel the need to write about their creator
or to pen myths that will explain our existence.
They search the skies for new life, and then
writers make science fiction for film
and print. They have mapped the skies,
know the alignment of the planets, and can
tell us why we can see them without
optical means. No need for new myths,
science is no longer fertile ground
for imaginative tales. There is little
strangeness in the sky for these sky-gazers,
just the possibility of a new planet and
new life as they search the sky with their telescopes.

Speed Limit

The new roadway snaked through
the communities on both sides,
taking some houses and small
firewood businesses with its stand.
The rivers of concrete moved
over the earth for several long
months until turning lanes
jutted from the concrete roadway
to the right and to the left into
the remaining subdivisions.
Motorists welcomed the newly
finished connection between
the state road and the historic one
with the 45 mph speed limit. A few
weeks after the roadway opened for drivers,
the discontent from the families
with shortened front lawns and
close location to the road registered
with city officials. A new speed
limit of 35 miles per hour resulted.
A policeman on duty for weeks failed
to convince the motorists to forget
the 45 mph speed limit. When he left
after a few weeks, the drivers resumed
their personal speed, zooming by those
who obeyed and darting from lane
to lane as if playing games of
"catch me if you can." Drivers' personal
speed limits now govern the road
with little regard or regret, and the
speed limit signs still post 35.

Sterile Visit

After a long wait,
the one in white I saw
for advice in the last week
was as impersonal as
the bored clerks I've seen
in department stores,
far more impersonal
than the stranger in black
at the back of the bus,
even less personal than
the cold voices on answering
machines. The whiteness of his
coat, like the stark white of
sunlight on new snow, deflected
my glances. Under white paper
tissues too small for cover,
my feelings, like blanched tomatoes,
lost their skins in the heart-cold
white sterility. He interrupted
my response to "Any problems?"
with pokes, taps, inserts, and commands
to open, to say "ah," to "breathe in, breathe
out. Bend." I left feeling at fault
for keeping the appointment.

Duplicity

The telling is the hard part,
not the forgetting. It's the telling
I mind, whether the milk is soured,
whether the eggs are fresh. Why so
much difficulty in telling the truth?
Does truth lie in brittle shells somewhere
out there while it appears on the chin
after breakfast? Look for it between
the bedsheets if you must, but don't nag me
about what we have left—just ourselves
and these shells of truth.

Too Often

I am listening *too often* to news
reports on public radio about violence
against citizens by policemen
in this country, including the
killing of a thirteen-year-old
with a toy gun in Cleveland. I feel
my legs turn to water *too often* and
the stone walls in my world collapse
too often, raining down shards of anger
and disbelief. I have to wonder why we
continue to argue *too often* over how
many angels can dance on the head
of a pin, when the young are dying
too often in the streets, *too often*
for no good reason.

Changing of Classes

Prattle.
Faint chatter.
Babble.
Rabble growing
behind closed doors,
rising and emerging
at the ringing.
Through doorways
pouring out,
one to two at first,
then en masse
like racehorses,
pounding.
Roaring voices
racing,
charging
along the walls,
sweeping
down the halls,
swelling en masse,
filling all space.
Quiet again
with the ringing.

Decision

The two first saw him in a country store.
They could hardly resist a touch.
They even picked him up. They checked
his tag. They put him back with his friends,
the cuddly bear, a yellow duck, rabbits,
puppies, and kittens, and walked away
to browse some more for one they'd adore more.
But his black and white softness, the deep
blue eyes, and the pink nose drew them back.
He was so cute, his black wool
against the white sheep's wool coat.
The couple came and left a second time,
leaving him behind, discussing
the pros and the cons:
Do we really want him?
Should we?
Does it matter the cost?
Three days before Christmas,
they brought him home, and two months later,
he sat alone, still and displayed, never
thinking that he might have a preference,
a choice he'd make different from their own.

The Subject of Beauty

Beauty is as beauty does, the grandmothers say.

For habit of confidence, she touches color to her lips
and powder to her shine and parades on stage.
She walks on cue, one mechanical foot before the other,
following the invisible social imprint.

Beauty is only skin deep, the grandmothers say.

And so the festivals repeat themselves
and the judges rate each beauty. One last question
to each decides all's fate. "This event is not so much
a beauty contest. We look for a girl's values," a spokesman explains.

Beauty lies in the eye of the beholder, the grandmothers say.

From appearances, judges find value
by looking to value beauty, like so much
common stock or precious metals.
Value can now be found in beauty.

Ad

About two weeks
into my twelfth
grade sewing class,
I opened my sewing
drawer to find my new pair
of dressmaker scissors
missing and in their place
a short fulcrum pair
that cut into my middle
finger when I cut fabric
by any pattern. It was a snub-
nosed pair, not blunt-nosed,
reminding me of a bulldog's face,
more like a pair of stunted snips
without a real purpose. I guessed
them to be a relative of a metal cutter,
a wire cutter, or a plumber's tool.
Their length of cut was very short,
a two-inch round cutting edge,
compared to the pointed
five-inch blades on the pair
that had been mine. No needle-sharp
points for accuracy and delicate
trimming in this strange pair. No one
admitted to have mistakenly stuck
my pair in a sewing drawer. Years later,
I took the pair out of the kitchen drawer
to trim some loose thread on a placement
mat and the slack between the levers
was too much for the job. Why else

have I kept these scissors over the years
but to write an ad to commemorate
their lack of worth and
to find their rightful owner?

Publishing Notes

I have lost that warm
and fuzzy feeling. I have
learned that poetry, one
of the oldest genres of time,
the living voice of the muses,
belongs to a lesser genre, has
a lesser god than other genres.
It warrants less respect for readability
in front matter than do other genres.
Pretty much anything goes
in the publication of poetry.
It lacks meaning and
sustenance when it comes to
making the big bucks. Everyone
in the know warns the poet,
"You won't get rich writing
poetry." This point brings me
to the question about respect for art.
Where is the respect for those who
plant the seeds? Who guards
the trees where the hearty
harvest the fruit from the trees?
I request that you, Reader, become
the reader of a poet's work. Then you
will come to know the respect
that flows from the poet to the genre,
conveying a truth you may forever
hold close to your heart
in your own breast pocket.

Ampersand

I have lost my place
among the twenty-six.
I have been kept in outer rooms
of stacked pages through the years,
waiting to rejoin the group,
for someone beyond the curtain
to invite me to the stage
to perform on the modern page.
Artisans have combined the *E* and *T*
to enhance the use and beauty.
Nothing has eased the
loneliness or misunderstanding
except for being swept up
by the designer's pen to the names
of businesses to live again.
I spend my time roaming
through the stacks
of pages to survive, to lessen
the loneliness. I began this life
as graffiti on a piece of stone
that survived the eruption
of Vesuvius in Pompeii.
I am sure only of my existence.

Drive By

I have driven by your house several times
a week after lunch for the past month.
It is a modern weathered architectural
structure, but I see nothing inviting
in the façade of your home. The house sits
dark and inattentive, no clue
to anyone's presence inside. It does seem
strange that after all these years I am not
comfortable stopping to knock on your door.
Friends we are, others may say.
I remember the times we shared lunch
on the job and discussed the budgets and
office plans. We always had plenty
to talk about on the job. Yet I continue
to drive past your place with thoughts
of how and what you are doing. I cannot see any
changes in landscaping, no new plants
or bed designs. In fact, I do not see one blooming
plant in the yard. Actually, your home looks
deserted, but I know someone warm is inside.
I should call you, maybe tomorrow.

Second Opinion

The rag doll has a highly developed
sensitivity to language, and he speaks quietly
as if afraid he will be a bother. He turns
his head from side to side with ears twitching
as he listens to spoken words. He comes and goes
whenever asked like a well-trained canine.
He honors the command "Stay" without
argument. In a cloud of calmness,
he leads the way to the kitchen
when hungry, checking with glimpses
backward, no meows, to make sure
he is followed. He is not a lap cat,
but he is very affectionate, kissing the hand
that feeds him. In the newly tiled master bath,
he has gone into the shower and has stretched
up, like the gymnast he is, to touch the decorative
glass tile, indicating his approval with serenity.
How nice to have a second opinion!

Grooming Glove

The cool fall breezes drape the morning
in calmness. The day's activities begin
slowly as if the beginning cycle
of a Ferris wheel and change rapidly
like the ride in bumper cars as the day's events collide.
This tight routine occurs each day. The
grooming attendant needs only to show him
the purple grooming glove and he comes
running like a child for the arms
of a favorite grandparent. As the
grooming glove moves through the
thick long hair inherited from his
Persian parent and over his body,
he falls into the trance of Bastet's songs
and drifts off to dreamland, rolling over
on his back in complete trust and exposing
his white underside resembling
peaked whipped cream. Without warning,
he jumps up with roller coaster speed on the
downward swoop and hurries over to his owner,
rubbing against the chair and kissing the hand
that reaches for him as if to say thanks.

Lost Garbage Can

A garbage can is not a pretty thing
with its gray larger-top-than-bottom design.
But it does cause consternation when it leaves
the yard and the owner cannot find it.

Like an adventurous child, the receptacle may
travel three to six houses away from its home
in the cul-de-sac to visit, making it difficult
without a honing device to find its way back.

While held in wide acclaim by owner, most neighbors do
not seem to care much about the lost garbage can.
Late afternoon the cans often end up bunched together
at the end of the cul-de-sac like neighbors in a friendly chat.

Once they break apart, getting the attention
of the recognizable one of them with a whistle
is also difficult. The one left does not look familiar.
Suffering from neglect and abuse, like a homeless

smelly, dirty drunk, it has all kinds of particles
stuck to its insides. Sometimes it too can disappear
and end up behind someone else's closed garage
door. A call to the city office to declare

the can lost gets sympathetic promises of replacement
that often wander too. Whether lost or damaged,
the can causes the same degree of anxiety
for the owner. With another call to the city office,

the homeowner learns he is a not the owner because
the can is owned by a private company, not
requiring that it be returned to its home
as the loyal family had expected.

Shared Grief

He has searched throughout the house
and has slept in every room as if
to capture her spirit passing. The days
have dragged behind the sun and
blended the months of longing
together. The sun now settles lower
in the western sky for the fall
season. Shutters on the windows
keep the sun remnants from
streaming in. The myrtles have
finished blooming, dropping their
blooms and leaves for the winter sleep.
Only a few cannas keep up the pace.
It was a string of utterances this morning
like no other heard from him that interrupted
my loneliness and continued for
several minutes. He had not been
himself, slower and less energetic
that morning, as he led me
to the bedroom where she had slept,
lifting a gentle paw to the closet door
for admittance. He went into her
apartment stored there. His grief,
like mine, comes and goes. He seems
to be doing well, but this behavior
reveals the slow progress of his pain.
At night he walks his grief and calls to her.
He looks longingly out the window
to the streets, hoping she will come back home
as she always did. We share this grief
as we always will.

Conundrum

Water seeks the lowest level,
where it becomes one with, or
swells to rise in backwash.
So it is with the trickling gurgle
from the water closet,
faint and slow. The fixture
has long dripped, gurgled,
murmured its loss. Exhausted,
it trickles down the porcelain sides,
dripping, dribbling, rolling to drain,
trickling, gurgling like promises
that strain the emotions
that stain the future and
weaken the structure.
Long deluged by drips, dribbles,
floods, of unexpressed feelings,
the sane with the insane,
sensitive with the insensitive,
tortured sensibilities
wearing away the porcelain face
like Chinese water torture.
Finally reaching the ebb
in time until, in flux, it surges
unexpectedly like backwash—
I am never quite sure.
Like moving water, I too seek
the lowest level where I become one with
or swell to rise in backwash.
Finally for what?
What does it matter but to me?

The Norm

E pur si muove.
—Galileo

There are no facts, only interpretations.
—Friedrich Nietzsche

I watch the mesmerizing
revolution as the blades move
in such deliberate ways
as to cause deliberations
in my head. The whims,
the forces of change,
the what that makes all
one and the same.
What source? How so
the revolution in me?
Now! Here in the bowl
on the kitchen counter.
Flour, sugar, butter,
eggs, and milk spin,
whirling and blending,
pulled outward in circles,
swirling valleys and ridges,
forming oracles of the germane
and the holy of this birthday cake.
Each swirl conscribing more,
pulling all into the flow of power,
the sifting, shifting blend in frenzy.
Oh, to be only a grain waiting for
a mischievous force to wash me away,
to cleanse me free of mind,
to swab me with the butter of time,

grain for grain,
scruple for scruple,
scripture for scripture.
Only the blend ever remains,
conformity to the norm,
originality shunned
as powdery facts and timely power
become one like the seed and the pulp,
the yolk and the albumen,
flour, sugar, butter, eggs, milk,
now in this bowl.

Nights of Mythic Fantasies

"What is black and white and read all over?"

In the early evening, the three would
gather on the porch of the house located
in the middle of the block. There, the three
widows in their loneliness would spin their
dreams in the cool summer breezes. Most
evenings a youngster joined them to listen
to their talk of life and mythic fantasies.
The three gained real purpose in guiding
this young one who came to visit: finishing school,
helping parents, and doing good. The celebration
for each visit was Dr. Pepper ice cream floats
and slices of iced cake. As the darkness crept over
the street and the front porch, the three widows would
call it a night. The young listener would go home
with the one who was her kinfolk, the Riddle Maker,
who would come alive telling riddles to the youngster
in the time left before sleep and dreams. When she left
the group for college, the young one slipped the riddles
and fantasies into a tote sack with her other memories
and took them with her to begin her new life.

Barry Cox's Church of Live Trees

The copper sheen has become
a venerable part of this living artistic
church. Its limbs trained on metal
have become an airy, rain-penetrable
church of green, brown, and purple leaves
forming the shape of the old stone churches
with pitched roofs that dot the countryside.
A fragile tree in a strong wind, it bends
and follows the metal without complaining
and needs primping before prime time.
Its personality is one of flexibility and
cooperation, because it understands
that there is protection in number from angry
winds for its gnarly but delicate limbs
and trunk in this holy church. The copper
sheens now channel from their chancel to their
friends, letting all know about the personal
cocoon, personal sanctuary for all.

Questions Still

It was the surprise that swept down
to seize my heart in its talons. Inside the chapel,
the body rested, lying so straight as if waiting.
My hand reached out to touch and brushed instead
the sleeve of the gray suit jacket, much coarser
than expected. On its journey, the hearse sped
over the hilly countryside without thinking
of its guest. The driver seemed to be listening
to hard rock as the hearse sped, bumping
and bouncing along the road. At the gravesite,
the fresh clay mound rose in the center
of the other markers. Heavy, humid silence
gathered its patience and settled down
around the edges to the corners of the opening.
Attendees in trance moved to the chairs around the edge
of the grave. The sentinel pines stood, respectfully
as soldiers in review, ready to deliver their
twenty-one gun salute. The words of the preacher
collected in a choking knot in my throat,
and I whispered, "Why?"

Pride

I willingly wish
to refrain from the tears
before they render
my feelings numb.
Over and over,
I run the feelings,
remembering,
focusing,
understanding,
freezing it
in permanence
selfishly
to bolster self
until the joy
escapes my heart's snare
in a tear down my cheek.

The Need to Pace

The need
to pace
is closely
related
to the need
to trace
one's thoughts
from emotion.
The feet move
in stride
like lead
along
tracing paper
to the resolution
that takes form.

Figment

I saw you on the TV last night.
There, in a moment's glance,
your presence blended for a split second
with that of the actress on screen.
The summons was fleetingly pleasant
but short. This morning I watched your car
cross the intersection ahead. My heart rose
needlessly. Again this afternoon, my mind
created your presence from the faint fragrance
of Aliage. Just now, I heard your voice.
Turning to look, I realized, *I've missed you.*

A Sight to See

The truck pulls out
of the driveway.
A closer look reveals
two who, at first, appear
to be young ladies.
They are sitting very
erect, prim and proper,
behind their chauffer as he
rounds the corner in his
four-seater truck. Then I see
that their ears substitute for golden
hair and their snouts are just
a little long for the beauties
they are in dog terms.
What a sight to see!
I wonder if they think of
themselves as characters
in *Driving Miss Daisy*.

Fickle Success

She declines
my invitation
to sit for tea
and cookies, to join
the daily prattle
about the weather.
She refuses to be
bought with nickels
and dimes, to be dined
on my self-pity or pain,
to be courted by kindness
and reason, or charmed
by empty promises.
Fickle Success prefers
the arm of Luck.

Miss Molly

Under the cloak of
dusk, she with her
freshly washed black
hair would head out
under stealth cover.
She was a roamer who
took her love to town
nightly, her blue-black hair,
her telling trait. Sometimes
she was gone for days,
returning none the worse,
and neighbors would say
that she was last seen down
the street visiting. She was
secretive and never disclosed
her rendezvous. When she
came to live with me
in the city, it was a big
change for her that
gave her more of the
life she had always
wanted. She did not
roam the neighborhood
but watched out her window
each day as the neighbors'
grandchildren played.
She seemed content
to have her own room
nicely furnished with
comfortable sofa, TV,
and leather chair.
It was not but two
years later that her health

began to fail. Whether
or not she missed her
old life, no one will ever
know, and no one ever
heard a complaint. She
was always a lady in our eyes,
always a saint.

Chill

A chill
has come
over me.
Beginning low,
the news
climbed
my numbed body,
filling my heart
with fear and rage,
stilling my thoughts
in process.
I cannot warm myself these days
or come back to the day-to-day routines
when
another black person's senseless murder
is chilling me.

Sisterhood

Friends soothe our unexpressed feelings
like soft rain on warm nights,
smoothing our rough, parched surfaces,
knowing well the crusted edges.
They cradle our expressed feelings
without judgment, caring not which way
we swing or how intoxicated by the ideal
we fling emotion allowing us passage, all to reveal.
Friends receive our spoken thoughts
as if they were as stable as cobalt blue
on glazed porcelain, as gifts gently
placed for safekeeping in fragrant
drawers or knowingly displayed under
glass. From reflection thereof, we soar.

Ars Amoris and *Ars Poetica*

Listening to Bob Seger's
Midwestern growl from *Ride Out,*
I feel his songs freeing
my thoughts. It does my
soul good to hear his rootsy
rock and roll. His deep
introspection fits well with
my thoughts today. I want
to ride the whitecapped waves
and climb the prophetic mountaintops
to watch sparring shards of light
in mirror glass, marvel at the unsure
at the moment where the one began and
the other stopped, where the edge lies,
the telling fruit drops. Centuries
of rhetoric have buried from sight
woman's half of the world's gold,
forgotten the powerful relationship
between needle and thread, pen and ink,
cheese and bread. Self-delusion
and reality, the twin of that between
which time spreads like fire, when
question and answer merge for self,
one with the seam between love and lust.
Between terrible and tender, fire and ice,
wind and tide, greed and need lie. It may
take me a lifetime to find the line between
mystery and ambiguity, the absurd and the comic.

The Muse Spurned

The student said, "We are studying
the poets—the four great ones."
(*Only four. I should think there
are more.*) "I don't know about poets,"
he continued. "Seems you have to have
a tragic childhood or to experience
terrible personal loss to be a poet.
I don't know. I can pass that up."
Catching his idea in the moment again,
he added, "And when you're ninety, they finally
recognize you with fame and money,
but then who needs it!"
I threw back my head to laugh,
but I had forgotten why. For those
too jaded before their time
will never drink the poetic wine
and will die cold sober.

From the Corner of My Eye

The shadow unfurls
the cosmic haze
of blue gauzed light,
and slithers of silence
flicker fire-blue
in neon flight.
From the divide to conscious order
through a doorway in time, you appear,
now visible and tissue-thin,
an amalgam of past diggings,
of ignored mental ruins,
unearthed and spiderwebbed,
tagged and racked.
I should know you,
faint remembrance
of sun and sky, stars and night,
riding the cool breezes
of my mind and disappearing
beyond the flight of the moment.
From the nebulous membrane
of permanence you evolve—
and vanish as quickly—
beyond memory's moment.
Static the day the brain turns
on stem and senses the disorder
in a passing blue shadow.
Semblance brushes against
the subtle verdigris
hindsight casts, and still
I dismiss your sudden appearance,
casual and unexpected
as a patch of early morning fog.
The mind's veil breaks and falls

like black velveteen draping the chill,
a mere brush fibrous and tentative
as cotton candy. In and out of the time
waltz, semblance dances and fades.

Moments in a Day

steam rising
from the iron pot on the trivet
announcing teatime

squares of candy
in Ghirardelli chocolate
stroke a warm heart

mailbox stacked full
evoking joy on holiday
for a tree of cards

ceramic tree on bar
glistening with lights galore
art aglow

the lights at the base
bathe the fiber optic tree
in the primary colors

squeals erupting
from toddler listening to poems
from *Goodnight Moon*

the black-and-white cat
crossing the lawn without fear
strolls with pride

Printed in the United States
By Bookmasters